ABOVE: *English quilt, pieced, applied and embroidered, dated 1797.*

COVER: *Horse armour in pieced patchwork quilted*

PATCHW(

Pamela Clat

Shire Publications Ltd

GW00600731

50p

CONTENTS

Introduction 3
Patchwork styles and methods 5
Patchwork in the USA 13
Patchwork in Britain 19
Patchwork in Africa and Asia 23
Patchwork in war and times of stress 26
Twentieth-century patchwork 29

Copyright © 1983 by Pamela Clabburn. First published 1983. Shire Album 101. ISBN 0 85263 631 8.
All rights reserved. No part of this publication may be reproduced or transmitted in any form or by any means, electronic or mechanical, including photocopy, recording, or any information storage and retrieval system, without permission in writing from the publishers, Shire Publications Ltd, Cromwell House, Church Street, Princes Risborough, Aylesbury, Bucks HP17 9AJ, UK.

Set in 9 on 9 point Times roman and printed in Great Britain by C. I. Thomas & Sons (Haverfordwest) Ltd, Press Buildings, Merlins Bridge, Haverfordwest, Dyfed SA61 1XE.

ACKNOWLEDGEMENTS

My best thanks are due to those who have so kindly lent me articles to photograph and made helpful suggestions: Juliet Webster of The Quiltery, Jeannie Millward of Country and Eastern, Hester Bury of Warner and Sons; Anna Wilson, Edith Gadsby and Ruth Lambert. The Victoria and Albert Museum, the American Museum in Britain, the Whitworth Art Gallery, the Museum of Mankind, Strangers Hall Museum and the National Trust have all been very helpful. Photographs are acknowledged as follows: American Museum in Britain, pages 7, 14 (lower), 15, 16; Country and Eastern, pages 10 (lower), 23; Museum of Mankind, front cover, page 24; National Trust, Blickling Hall, pages 8 (top), 26; National Trust, Cragside, pages 10 (top), 32; National Trust, Wallington, page 8 (lower); Norfolk Museums Service, page 6 (top), 27, 28; Jill Salmon, page 22; Shakespeare Memorial Theatre, page 21; Victoria and Albert Museum, pages 1, 2, 3, 6 (lower), 9 (lower), 17, 18, 20; Warner and Sons Ltd, page 4; Whitworth Art Gallery, Manchester, page 25.

Cotton cover for a hackney carriage in applied patchwork. India, c 1869.

Pieced Welsh quilt in which the quilting is more important than the patchwork. Last quarter of the nineteenth century.

INTRODUCTION

Patchwork would appear to be at least as old as the book of Genesis, which says that 'Israel loved Joseph more than all his children . . . and he made him a coat of many colours.' This was possibly goatskin, possibly dyed homespun linen: we do not know, but there at this very early date is the idea that garments of many colours are beautiful and a labour of love, and this idea has continued until today.

The craft of patchwork, sometimes raised to an art, consists of cutting up pieces of material, old and new, and rejoining them in pattern to make a whole fabric which can be used for many purposes, from bed coverings to pincushions.

Patchwork has generally been the response to a need or a wish to be economical, to use up scraps and offcuts of fabric and make the good parts of several articles such as old dresses into something new and attractive. In the *Reminiscences of a Gentlewoman of the Last Century* (the eighteenth) Miss Hutton says she was promised 'a calico bed-quilt that was a gown and petticoat of my grand-mother's' — most likely made from imported Indian fabrics. But from the eighteenth century to the present day, new fabric also, often in small quantities cut for the purpose, has been bought to eke out older pieces. For example, in the *Diary of a Country Parson* James Wood-

Design for a roller-printed fabric simulating patchwork, produced by Warner and Sons, 1929.

forde notes in 1789 that he bought '1 yard of different kinds of cotton for patchwork for my Niece', and in 1790 he records: 'To 16 Half Quarters of cotton for Patches 0.5.0. which last I gave to my Niece for her work.' The many other cotton materials he bought would all have provided offcuts for Nancy's piece bag. In the nineteenth century in the United States, when women in isolated districts had run short of pieces they or their husbands bought bolts of brightly coloured cloth to use, and in the twentieth century swatches of sample fabrics and remnants from drapers, bundles specially made up and even expensive cottons bought by the yard have all been used avidly by the many women in all countries enjoying the craft.

Patchwork has never completely died out; at times it has been either more or less fashionable but there have always been revivals, perhaps in a different form, as, for example, the fashion for crazy patchwork in the late nineteenth century. The present revival, which has had a great impetus since the Second World War, may be said to have started in the 1920s and was even then sufficient to encourage the fabric firm of Warners in both 1929 and 1930 to produce a cotton designed and printed to resemble patchwork. This type of fabric had been produced as early as the 1860s, which may well be forgotten when looking at the dozens of similar designs produced today.

When discussing patchwork it is difficult to omit quilting as so often the crafts are linked, but they each stand in their own right as distinct and separate. There are many bedcovers made in patchwork which are not quilted or which are quilted but not patched. Smaller objects made in patchwork are seldom quilted.

Quilting was added to patchwork when warmth was required. An interlining, which might be sheep's wool, an old blanket, a worn-out patchwork quilt, or today a light terylene wadding, was placed between the new top and the lining and then the three thicknesses were sewn together with running stitches in pattern. These patterns might echo or follow the patchwork design or they could be quite different shapes, formed from feathers, wine glasses, swags, lozenges or other simple designs.

PATCHWORK STYLES AND METHODS

There are many styles of patchwork, which vary according to the materials available, the object to be made and the preferred type of design. The sewing techniques vary accordingly, but they are all based on two main types: applied and pieced. Both these originated centuries ago and the main difference is that applied relies on small motifs cut from one or more fabrics sewn on to a ground, while pieced consists of small pieces sewn together making one whole fabric. In a number of articles these two methods are mixed.

APPLIED PATCHWORK

In working applied patchwork, motifs from decorative fabrics are cut out, the edges turned under and hemmed or slip-stitched on to a ground fabric. Alternatively the edges can be left raw and the motifs sewn down with buttonholing. In the eighteenth and early nineteenth centuries applied patchwork was considered superior to pieced work, needing more accurate cutting, neater sewing and a more expert eye for the planning and balance of the motifs. Certainly the bedcoverings still to be seen of this date, using motifs cut from chintzes, particularly the favourite Palm and Pheasant, are among the most beautiful pieces known.

PIECED PATCHWORK

Pieced patchwork differs from applied in that a strong fabric has to be made from small pieces. This, having no ground material, needs to be lined because of all the raw edges at the back. Two main techniques have been evolved, one general in Britain and the other more usual in the United States.

In the first, pieces of stiff paper are cut to use as templates. The fabric, cut a little larger, is tacked over the templates and the units are joined together by oversewing, after which the papers are removed. However, there are many pieces to be found in which the papers are still present. Sometimes this is because the fabric used has been silk or velvet, both unwashable in this context, so the papers can be left in as a stiffening, but more often it seems that the article is unfinished and the worker has baulked at removing the thousands of small pieces of paper. Occasionally a piece can be dated from these scraps, which are often cut from old letters and envelopes.

In the United States paper templates are not used. The fabric is cut and creased and then the pieces are joined with running stitches. As one process is left out and running is quicker than oversewing the American method is much faster. This helps to explain why the American patchworker seems able to make so many more quilts than her British counterpart.

LOG CABIN

Log cabin patchwork is also called American log, Canadian log or ribbon work. Although, as its various names imply, this type of patchwork was and is worked on the American continent it is also found in Britain as well as Afghanistan, the Middle East and Portugal. It is an obvious technique for using up small scraps of cloth or ribbon and is built up in the same way as the logs are piled in the log cabins of America. Some quilts from Sind in Pakistan have log cabin and

ABOVE: *Detail of an applied quilt using motifs from the Palm and Pheasant chintz. Dated in cross stitch 1805 and 1821.*

BELOW: *Pieced and applied bedcover in which the border leaves imitate the feather pattern used in quilting. English, mid nineteenth century.*

American quilt using the Fan pattern in blocks. 1930s.

pieced work combined in an overall pattern.

A small square of fabric is tacked to the foundation cloth and then narrow strips of material are sewn on with running stitch along each side of the square in turn until a block of the requisite size is made. By distributing the colours in the block so that one half is dark and one half light and then joining the blocks in different ways various ingenious patterns can be built up, based entirely on tone value. In late nineteenth-century England there was a vogue for what were known as 'ribbon quilts', made in the same technique but using short lengths of the ribbons used for trimming hats instead of fabric.

SHELL OR CLAM SHELL

This method has been used only infrequently, probably because it needs a more competent needlewoman than other methods and does not readily lend itself to pattern making. The shell shape has always been popular in embroidery and never more so than in the mid eighteenth century, when it was a favourite quilting design, so it was perhaps natural to try to translate it into patchwork. The shape of the patch used is a convex semicircle at the top, curving to two concave quarter circles at the bottom. Each convex top is turned under and tacked. When a row of these patches is placed together it will be seen that the concave sides of adjoining patches form a semicircle and it is to these that the convex side of the next row of patches is sewn. Patterns can only be made by placing the patches in rows, so there is very little scope for design and the technique is more suitable for small objects than large.

The lower illustration on page 9 shows part of a set of eighteenth-century bedhangings in the Victoria and Albert Museum. The lack of design definition has been overcome by sewing ribbon over the joins in diagonals.

CRAZY OR PUZZLE PATCHWORK

This was very popular on both sides of the Atlantic in the second half of the nineteenth century. It admirably filled the demand for needlework which was simple but rich and showy. It required a foundation fabric, which could be any old unwanted sheeting or other material. To

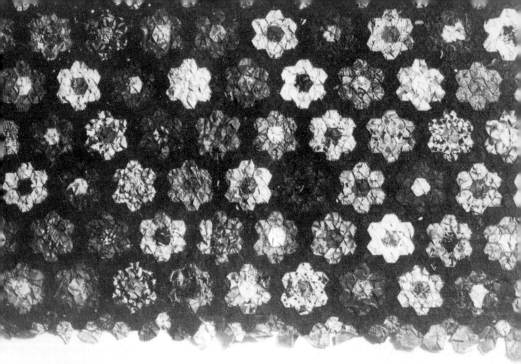

ABOVE: *The back of an unfinished English pieced patchwork with the papers removed. Nineteenth century.*

BELOW: *A quilt in log-cabin technique, made in Yorkshire, late nineteenth century.*

 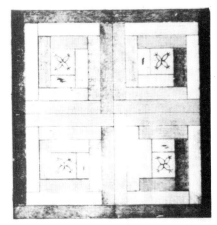

ABOVE: *Log-cabin technique described in Weldon's 'Practical Patchwork', c 1890.*

BELOW: *One of a set of four bed curtains in printed cotton in shell pattern. The extreme busyness of the design is corrected by the green ribbon which outlines the lozenge-shaped blocks. English, late eighteenth century.*

ABOVE: *Tablecloth of silks and velvets in crazy patchwork. English, late nineteenth century.*
BELOW: *Detail of a bedcover in alternate blocks of crazy patchwork and embroidered silk. Early twentieth century.*

A cushion in cathedral windows technique by Edith Gadsby, 1981.

this were tacked pieces of silk, velvet, brocade or ribbon, higgledy-piggledy, but each overlapping. All these tacked pieces were then fastened to each other and the foundation with feather stitch or herringbone, generally worked in a golden-yellow twisted thread. Sometimes individual patches were embroidered.

In 1885 J. L. Patten of New York sold mail order kits for crazy patchwork. For 35 cents he supplied 'Ten sample pieces of elegant silk, all different, and cut out so as to make a diagram showing how to put them together, and a variety of new stitches'. There is nothing new!

CATHEDRAL WINDOWS

This type of patchwork is now very popular. It originated in the United States among the Mennonites and is now practised in both America and Britain. It needs fairly large pieces of non-fraying firm fabric. These pieces are folded and creased into double 'envelopes', which are oversewn together. A small piece of a different design is placed over the join and then the top folds of the envelope are turned back and sewn down on to it. The result is an attractive series of four-petalled flowers on a different ground.

QUILL, SOMERSET AND FOLDED PATCHWORK

In each of these styles small pieces of fabric are folded into quills and sewn individually to a ground fabric. Quill patchwork was described in *Practical Patchwork,* one of Weldon's magazines of the 1890s, and was recommended as a method of using up all scraps of any type of fabric in any colour. The ground was ticking so that the folded pieces of fabric could be sewn to the stripes. The quills, folded so as not to show any raw edges, stood upright, resembling the fashionable button rugs of the time.

Somerset patchwork developed in Canada and also relied on folded fabric forming quills, but these were crisp and sewn flat in pattern to a ground fabric.

ABOVE: *Four cushions by Juliet Webster in different techniques, 1981: (left to right, at back) shell, cathedral windows, Seminole; (in front) folded patchwork.*

LEFT: *Cushion in Seminole technique by Anna Wilson, 1981.*

Folded patchwork is a modern variation using much the same technique as Somerset.

PATCHWORK ON THE MACHINE

Before the advent of the sewing machine in the 1850s and for many years after all patchwork was done by hand. In some cases time was important, but generally the craft was looked on as a relaxation. Also in Britain, using the paper template and overcasting technique it was not possible to substitute machine for hand work. In America it was different as the running stitches used to join the pieces could be put in by machine as well as by hand. So where there was urgency the machine began to be used. It is therefore not surprising that the first type of patchwork designed specifically to be worked on the sewing machine should have come from the USA.

SEMINOLE PATCHWORK

The Seminoles are a tribe of American Indians who originally lived in Georgia. After a series of wars against the white man the remnants of the tribe settled in Florida in the 1880s. Here, possibly influenced by the American patchwork they saw, they decorated their clothes with an unusual type they created on the sewing machine. First, strips of different patterned and plain fabrics were joined by machine to make a whole fabric. Next, this fabric was cut across at an angle in strips. Then these strips could be rearranged into many different patterns according to taste and machined together.

Straight stitching on the machine does not offer many other possibilities but the advent of the swing needle has suggested more variations. One method, introduced by Julia Roberts, uses a combination of fabric pieces, iron-on vilene and the swing needle. A piece of iron-on vilene is cut slightly larger than the finished article and the pieces, cut to exact size, are pinned carefully and accurately to it and are then slowly ironed on. The pieces are next joined with swing-needle stitching, making the stitching into part of the design. This results in a slightly stiffened, attractive article, but there is no margin for error, and though quick by hand-sewn standards it is not a relaxing form of patchwork.

PATCHWORK IN THE USA

In a country as vast as the United States in which over the past three centuries people have experienced the extremes of great wealth and great poverty, it is not surprising that patchwork in many forms should vary from a hobby for the rich to a bleak necessity and almost a way of life for the pioneer poor.

But the United States is peopled by families who came mainly from Europe and largely from Britain, bringing their skills, knowledge and background with them. From these varied cultures came differing styles of patchwork, but also from them there evolved a type instantly recognisable as American. This was generally worked by women who moved westwards with their husbands in the nineteenth century looking for land, and who had to be completely self-reliant, producing every necessity. The land and the weather were harsh and unaccommo-dating and warmth and colour were not only pleasurable but were stark necessities if the families were to survive. So these women sat whenever they had a spare moment piecing small bits of fabric from the bit bag they had brought with them and making quilts of great beauty. As with all the best craftsmanship, the quilts were firstly completely functional and only secondly were they beautiful.

Far more often than in Britain did they design using a block and sett, that is, making a series of identical patterns about 12 inches (300 mm) square (the blocks) and setting them into a frame of fabric about 2 inches (50 mm) wide of a contrasting colour which joined to the next block. This scheme gives great clarity to the design, and as the setts are made from straight strips there is not so much piecing and time is saved.

An almost unlimited number of pat-

terns can be made in this way and they varied from state to state, being based on local scenes such as windmills, pine trees, flying birds and animals. Some patterns became great favourites and were made in many places, apparently changing their names at each state boundary.

The West then consisted of small townships far apart, each serving a rural hinterland. This isolation encouraged a strong feeling of community, with people standing together against the harsh condi-

LEFT: *Sampler of block and sett.*

BELOW: *American quilt with the popular Sunburst design and an applied border. Nineteenth century.*

An Amish pieced quilt from Milton, Iowa, using a mixture of cotton and woollen fabrics, 1920s.

tions, and from this feeling sprang a particular type of quilt known as Album or Friendship. In these each block was designed and made by a different person and the quilt was finished and quilted by the community and then given to someone loved and respected such as a retiring minister or doctor or an engaged girl. These quilts were much prized by the recipient and little used and so are often in immaculate condition today.

Some settlers, especially those with strong religious views, kept their own recognisable style of quilt making, the best known being the Amish. These are a branch of the Mennonites from Switzerland and the lower Rhine and like the Shakers they eschew ornament and gaiety. The result is that their quilts are distinguished by the use of large pieces of plain fabric in unusual bold though subtle colour combinations with exquisite stitching.

However, not all American quilts were beautiful. Up to twenty were needed to produce enough warmth to keep alive in the bitterly cold winters and some were very rough and ready, but there was

Fan quilt in a mixture of blocks and crazy patchwork, with additional embroidery. Late nineteenth century.

Man's dressing gown in chiné and plain silks. English, late nineteenth century.

usually a top quilt made with great care using the best pieces of fabric and this one gave colour and beauty to the often cheerless surroundings.

In the eighteenth and early nineteenth centuries many superb quilts were made in the great colonial houses. Rich and cultured ladies, helped by dependants and slaves, made quilts which were often applied, using at first imported cottons and chintzes and later materials woven from cotton grown in the southern states. These bedcovers closely resembled those being made in Britain at the same time.

A different type of quilt was made in Hawaii, now one of the United States. Patchwork is not indigenous there as there had been no necessity for it, but missionaries took both the craft and bolts of cloth to the islands and the Hawaiians quickly learned to make their own versions of the quilt. They used only two contrasting colours and their designs were formed by folding paper into four and cutting a pattern. The results sometimes resemble giant snowflakes and have form and beauty without the restlessness often apparent in American designs.

Quilt in applied patchwork. English, early nineteenth century.

Four pincushions showing great variety in size and style. The large one is pieced felt stuck with pins and bears the legend 'Remember me'; it was probably made by a soldier or sailor. Small cushions from left to right: pieced diamonds in cotton; jockey cap in silk with pins down the seams; and silk squares pieced and stuck with pins in pattern.

PATCHWORK IN BRITAIN

Although it is known that patchwork, both pieced and applied, was made in Britain in the middle ages our detailed knowledge of the craft begins with the bed hangings made for Levens Hall in 1708. These consist of large octagonal, cruciform and church window motifs made from imported Indian chintzes applied on a white ground. The confidence with which they had been made and the remark in *Gulliver's Travels* (published in 1726) that Gulliver's clothes made by the Lilliputians 'looked like the patchwork made by the ladies of England' suggest that patchwork was then enjoying a revival.

References to the craft are few until the last quarter of the eighteenth century, when both Parson Woodforde and Miss Hutton mention it, Miss Hutton adding that she had 'made patchwork beyond calculation'. In 1780 Mrs Lybbe Powys in her memoirs refers to a 'Miss Hudson (who teaches the new patchwork in Bath)'. This might have been shell patchwork.

At the end of the eighteenth century bed hangings and coverings were made by the well-to-do and poor alike, varying in complexity with the ease with which fabrics and time were available. In general applied work was done by those who had access to the fashionable chintzes, while pieced quilts were made by both rich and poor.

Among the many counterpanes made in the early nineteenth century were commemorative ones. These sometimes had a series of vignettes round the border or had a specially printed centrepiece commemorating such national events as George III's Golden Jubilee in 1810 or the Duke of Wellington's victory at Vittoria in 1813. These centrepieces, which

19

Detail of a pieced and applied quilt. The piecing of the melon-shaped fabrics is patchwork of the highest order. The border shows vignettes of army and domestic life. English, c 1805.

might also be printed with nothing more than a basket of flowers, were often applied on top of pieced work rather than being let in. This raises the question as to whether they were sometimes used to modernise an older quilt.

The craft increased in popularity in the nineteenth century, being used for innumerable small items as well as bedcovers. The fabric generally chosen for hard wear was cotton, which was bright and pretty, had good washing qualities and, because of its firm weave, was easy to use. Silks, satins and velvets were made into more decorative articles. Writing in the *Ladies Manual of Fancy Work* in 1859, Mrs Pullan, a great arbiter of fashionable handwork, says of patchwork: 'This is a favourite amusement with many ladies, as by it they convey useless bits of silk, velvet or satin into really handsome articles of decoration. Of the patchwork with calico I have nothing to say. Valueless indeed must be the time of that person who can find no better use for it than to make ugly counterpanes and quilts of pieces of cotton.'

One woman who worked against the general mainstream was Mrs Harris of Stratford-upon-Avon. She composed pictures of her native town, basically pieced, but with embroidered and applied decoration. Her compositions are accurate in detail and show how much life and interest can be given to what is often a very formal medium.

The writer of *Practical Patchwork*, a magazine of the early 1890s, like Mrs Pullan thirty years earlier, suggests that patchwork has at last outgrown its 'childishness' and become a favourite work, especially when done in silks and velvets. She also refers to hospital quilts 'made of good-sized squares of red twill and white calico, placed alternately, like the squares on a chess board, the white pieces having texts written upon them, or Scripture pictures outlined with marking ink; they are much appreciated and prove a great source of interest to the poor invalids.'

A panel depicting a house and shop in Stratford-upon-Avon. Pieced patchwork with some additional embroidery, worked by Mrs Harris in 1876.

A funerary shrine or 'nwomo' made by Udoh Unor Aran Ekat of the Annang Ibidio, Nigeria, in pieced and applied patchwork. Twentieth century.

In the North of England particularly, quilting clubs were formed by individual women as a method of making a little extra money to help the family finances without leaving the house. The quilts might be plain quilted or patched and quilted and the customers paid what they could afford each week towards the finished quilt. It was hard work for the sewer but was sometimes the only income when unemployment or illness hit the family. These clubs existed until the Second World War.

PATCHWORK IN AFRICA AND ASIA

Sewing is a craft not usually associated with Africa. However, in some areas, seemingly with little relation to one another, patchwork is found, and it is true patchwork as much as that of America or Britain.

The applied patchwork of Egypt has been well known for centuries and is still a tourist attraction. Figures cut from coloured linens or cottons march across a ground fabric in never ending procession.

In North Africa there are two other distinct styles. The first is the protective armour for horse and man worn by the tribesmen of the Sudan. The pieced patchwork in strong, bright colours, using squares and triangles for the design, is very much like the patchwork of Sind hundreds of miles to the north-east, and it seems probable that the style travelled from there to the Sudan by the camel and trade routes. The second type was worn by the officers in the army of the Mahdi, an Islamic religious leader. Originally his followers, devoted to a life of poverty, wore roughly patched beggars' *jibbehs*, which could scarcely be dignified by the name of patchwork. Later, these rough garments became formalised by the army officers into a white garment with applied patchwork of blue and brown — a long way from the original concept.

Further south, in Nigeria, patchwork is used for funerary shrines. These are ephemeral, being out of doors and only lasting as long as the weather will allow. They are professionally made and depict facets of the life of the deceased in applied patchwork surrounded by a pattern of pieced work.

A cover in pieced patchwork from Sind, quilted in straight lines. Twentieth century.

In South Africa an interesting experiment is being tried in Soweto. A self-help group, the Žamini Soweto Sisters, have been taught the ordinary American patchwork and are now starting to make their own designs. These have a strong African look which will probably become more pronounced as time goes on.

In that part of Asia which includes Iran, Afghanistan, Baluchistan and Sind there are many forms of patchwork, both pieced and applied, and there seems to be as long a tradition of the craft here as anywhere in the world. Iran was well

Cloth, possibly from the Ivory Coast, West Africa. The blue and white design, supposed to imitate tie-and-dye, bears a striking resemblance to some American patterns, for example 'cotton reel'.

Camel trapping in pieced patchwork made by the Turkmen tribe of north-east Iran.

known in the eighteenth and nineteenth centuries for the work produced in and around Resht on the Caspian Sea. This is sophisticated patchwork, far removed from folk art. It is sometimes pieced and sometimes applied and is embellished with cords and stitchery. The designs are flowing, with flowers, foliage and birds.

Not far from Resht the Turkmen tribes produce camel trappings in pieced patchwork, and both camel and horse trappings are made in various forms of patchwork throughout the whole area.

Katab work from Kathiawar, south of Sind, is, at its best, sophisticated. It is applied patchwork used frequently for large festival hangings, being quicker and cheaper to make than by using true embroidery. The background is a white cloth to which motifs of men, animals and trees are applied. Border patterns are cut as though to interlock in pieced patch-

work style but then small hems are turned under and stitched to the ground leaving a thread of white showing between the motifs. This last technique is also used in the *rilly* work of Sind. The word 'rilly' comes from an Urdu word meaning to mix and connect and is an exact definition of the work. Rillies are made in vast numbers in Sind. They are used as saddle cloths, for fashionable clothing, for export as quilts and as covers for virtually everything. They are particularly used by the Sufis, who, like the followers of the Mahdi, use patchwork as an expression of their religion. They make parts of their clothing — caps, jackets and *chaddars* — from scraps of fabric to show their humility and they use rillies as rugs so that at their religious festivals the whole ground is covered with brightly coloured patchwork cloths.

25

Detail of a quilted bedcover in a variety of patchwork techniques, both hand and machine sewn. One of the many hundreds sent to Britain by the Canadian Red Cross in 1942.

PATCHWORK IN WAR AND TIMES OF STRESS

Patchwork in war has been notable on two counts: the practical and the therapeutic. On the practical side it has frequently provided a covering for the quilted fabrics which, before the use of gunpowder, were often sufficient to withstand an arrow or turn the point of a spear. Mention has been made of the quilted and patched armour for horse and man of the Sudanese tribesmen and the officers in the army of the Mahdi. This was in comparatively modern times but in the middle ages patchwork was also used to single out individual commanders who would wear surcoats over their armour emblazoned with their coat of arms, which, together with their banners, provided a rallying point for their troops.

In the field of therapy the making of patchwork bedcovers has had a very practical role. The Royal College of Surgeons has a picture showing Private Thomas Wood sitting up in his hospital bed making a bedcover of triangular pieces. He was a patient at the time of the Crimean War and only one of many wounded men who have found the craft ideally suited to convalescence. It is equally well suited to the chronically sick and disabled. The pieces are light and easily handled, they are pleasant to look at and there is the fascination of a simple jigsaw puzzle and the promise of a useful and attractive article at the end.

Patchwork bedcovers have been extensively used for fund raising in war time, as in peace for various good causes. But they have been more valuable in war because of the comparative ease with which the fabrics could be procured. Cut-up garments and bit bag pieces were more easily acquired than new fabrics. Writing during the First World War in *Stitchery*, Flora Klickmann says: 'That useful branch of old-time needlework, the patchwork quilt, has been revived, and this revival is due to the exigency of economy during war time. The price of all materials being so very high, and the need for economy so great, have led to many useful devices, in order to maintain a reasonable amount of comfort during these trying times, and not the least of these is the patchwork quilt.' Those sentiments were also felt during the American Civil War, the Crimean War and the Second World War.

During the Second World War another type of patchwork quilt appeared. The Canadian Red Cross organised the making of these quilts, which were sent to Britain in bales to be used by members of

Bedcover made by the women prisoners in Newgate Prison under the supervision of Elizabeth Fry. Mid nineteenth century.

Bedhead and valance. Part of a complete bed in pieced and applied patchwork made by Mrs Brereton, c 1806.

the various women's forces to add brightness and warmth to their functional hutments. These quilts were of variable quality, some made in the normal way though plain rather than elaborate, some machined, and yet others an amalgam of bits and pieces with parts hand-stitched and other parts machined, as though the maker had taken trial pieces and odd bits from her friends and hastily put them together. Most were backed with primrose yellow cotton and all were very welcome.

One place in which patchwork provided a much needed therapy in times of great mental and physical stress was the women's prison at Newgate. Elizabeth Fry, the well loved prison reformer, held Bible classes for the inmates of this prison and also taught them the craft of patchwork and provided the necessary pieces. Many of these women were awaiting transportation and it is believed

that they took their patchwork with them to provide some relief on the long, frightening and insanitary journey. There may well still be relics of those spreads in Australia though it is probable that by now they are all in rags. A quilt made in Newgate and now in Stranger's Hall Museum in Norwich is illustrated. It has little artistic value but considering the conditions under which it was made it is a wonderful piece of work.

Mental illnesses such as melancholia have also benefited from the therapeutic qualities of patchwork. In 1806 Mrs Brereton of Norfolk was stricken after the deaths of her two sons, but eventually she was discovered fiddling with small pieces of fabric and these eventually became the complete furnishings for a bed, made over a period of years in both coffin-shaped and hexagonal pieces with some applied work. Happily this therapy brought her back to normality.

Tea cosy, pieced in the 'English country garden' style of the 1950s and 1960s.

TWENTIETH-CENTURY PATCHWORK

For much of the twentieth century up to the Second World War there was little interest in patchwork as a craft and still less as an art. This is not to say that none was being done, for there was a considerable amount being made in the old tradition. At the beginning of the century there was crazy patchwork and as always the craft revived in wartime. Fostered by the Women's Institutes, patchwork was taught in many villages in the 1920s and 1930s with a great emphasis on accurate technique and not very much on adventurous planning.

It was not until about the 1960s that there was an explosion in the craft and as in many other branches of embroidery patchwork has been given new life in both Britain and the United States by trained students with original ideas from the art schools and colleges. These gradu-ates, exploring all possibilities, draw the less adventurous after them until today there are groups of workers in many towns and villages who meet to exchange ideas and techniques. They are constantly expanding the craft in many ways. One is by trying the effect of fabrics which would have been frowned on in the past, such as corduroy, where the play of light on the ribs of the material gives a most decorative effect. Another way is by turning patchwork into soft sculpture with detached and padded pieces, in effect enlarging on trapunto quilting with patchwork.

Experiments in dyeing and spraying are taking place, not in the same way that a piece of fabric used to be dyed when there was not enough of a certain colour in the piece bag, but dyeing or spraying many pieces in varying shades possibly based on one colour.

A number of hangings are pictorial and lack the disciplined regularity of design so noticeable in many old quilts; unusual colour schemes are seen, and in some places the effect of light plays a large part, with fabrics being twisted and pleated.

Effects for use in church have been tried, in some cases with great success, and the pieces of jewel-like colour now found in altar frontals or on copes or chasubles complement and enhance grey stone pillars and stained glass windows. These may be sumptuous and by brilliant designers such as those by Beryl Dean for Westminster Hospital Chapel or Malcolm Lochhead for St Mungo's Cathedral in Glasgow or they may be on a smaller and humbler but no less effective scale for a village church.

All these ideas are derived from traditional patchwork: there is nothing wholly new in any of them, but the emphasis is different and in many cases more attractive to modern eyes.

Alongside the modern experimentalists are many people using old designs and making beautiful quilts. They are also resurrecting techniques forgotten or ignored since the nineteenth century, such as cathedral windows, Somerset and quill patchwork and Seminole work. Today this old craft has taken on a new lease of life and is in the forefront of modern creative needlework.

The back of a modern waistcoat with a panel taken from a late nineteenth-century silk quilt which was too worn for use. One patch says 'Morton 1888'. American.

Scaffolding. Panel by Ruth Lambert, 1980.

PLACES TO VISIT
Most museums have some patchwork but the largest collections are at:
The American Museum in Britain, Claverton Manor, Bath, Avon BA2 7BD.
  Telephone: Bath (0225) 60503.
Beamish: North of England Open Air Museum, Beamish, Stanley, County Durham
  DH9 0RG. Telephone: Stanley (0207) 31811.
Strangers Hall Museum, Charing Cross, Norwich, Norfolk NR2 4AL. Telephone:
  Norwich (0603) 611277 extension 275.
Victoria and Albert Museum, Cromwell Road, South Kensington, London SW7 2RL.
  Telephone: 01-589 637.
Welsh Folk Museum, St Fagans, Cardiff CF5 6XB. Telephone: Cardiff (0222) 569441.

FURTHER READING

Betterton, Shiela. *Quilts and Coverlets.* The American Museum in Britain, 1978.
Colby, Averil. *Patchwork.* 1958.
Cooper, P. and Buferd, N. B. *The Quilters.* Anchor Press/Doubleday, 1978.
Good Housekeeping. Patchwork and Appliqué. Ebury Press, 1981.
Irwin, J. and Hall, M. *Indian Embroideries.* S. R. Bustikar, Ahmedabad, 1972.
McCall's Book of Quilts. John Murray, 1964.
Picton, J. and Mack, J. *African Textiles.* British Museum Publications Ltd, 1978.
Safford, C. L. and Bishop, R. *America's Quilts and Coverlets.* E. P. Dutton, 1972.
Salmons, J. 'Funerary Shrine Cloths of the Annang Ibidio, South-East Nigeria'. *Textile
  History* volume 11, 1980.
Threadlines Pakistan. The Ministry of Industries, Government of Pakistan, 1977.

A bedcover in pieced patchwork based on the hexagon. English, nineteenth century.